# The Prepper's Long-Term Survival Guide & Off Grid Living

## A Complete Guide to Building Your Homestead and Becoming Self-Sufficient

**Michael Cowern**

# Introduction

For most people, living off-grid is synonymous with the life of a caveman. They think that all there is to off-grid living is wearing animal skin and cooking food on top of an open fire. Other people think it is isolating oneself in a log cabin out in the woods without communicating with society. However, is that really what it means to live a self-sufficient lifestyle?

In this book, we explain the fundamentals of living off the grid, its advantages and disadvantages, as well as how to get started on your own selfsufficiency journey. Our goal is to educate interested readers on the importance of building a self-sufficient lifestyle, especially with the current events happening in the world. It's always important to stay prepared for natural disasters and potential societal collapses. It's also important to completely rely on yourself when it comes to your own needs. Imagine how much of an impact you'll have on the overall carbon footprint when you ditch conventional fossil fuel-powered services and utilities.

There are many reasons to switch to off-grid living. For starters, the air is much cleaner outside of the city, so consider living off the land if your goal is to live healthy. You'll also enjoy complete privacy when you build your own home and disconnect from society. Yes, you can live in an off-grid community, but you'll still be able to live by your own rules without the intervention of any higher authority. Introverts will really enjoy this kind of life.

Also, sounds are much more pleasant outside the city. You can say goodbye to those noisy kids that wake you up every morning or the annoying car honks that ruin your afternoon. When you own the land you live on, the only sounds that will wake you up in the morning are the therapeutic sounds of nature. Who can possibly say no to that? This is why it's much easier to think when you live out in the wilderness. You're not just in a better mood, but you're also more relaxed and able to hear your own thoughts.

It can be a really empowering step to start looking after your own needs. Not just on a physical level but also on a mental and emotional level. You won't just escape the monotony of society's everyday life, but you'll also learn valuable lessons and have more confidence in yourself and your decisions. This book gives you all you need to have before you make the switch.

## Who Chooses the Off-Grid Lifestyle and Why?

While the modern "grid" is more advanced than any organizational structure in history, there are a range of reasons why people might choose to get off of the grid.

### *Preparing for the Worst*

While some people trust that the grid will take care of their basic needs for the rest of their lives, others aren't so sure. Repeated breakdowns of municipal services, such as the widespread power outages during Hurricane Ida in 2021, have resulted in many people deciding they would be better off looking after themselves.

Furthermore, the past few years have been unprecedentedly difficult for many Americans, considering the rising cost of living combined with the coronavirus pandemic. Many people are wondering if modern society as we understand it will survive, or if social unrest, climate change, and other disasters will result in a breakdown of social order. Going off-grid and becoming self-sufficient gives many people a peace of mind that no matter what happens, they'll be able to look after themselves and their families.

## Long-Term Savings and Escaping the Rat Race

While going off the grid is a significant investment, many people do realize producing their own food, water, and power would save a lot of money in the long run. As the cost of living in cities continues to rise, the idea of taking control of your own finances can sound extremely attractive.

Many people feel that work is taking over their lives. Not only are they working long hours, they're also driving long commutes, making workrelated activities take up most of the day. Many people stuck in this situation feel their lives are being sucked away from them and wish that they could spend more time outside experiencing nature.

The invention of smartphones and computers hasn't helped with work-life balance. As many workplaces still don't have "right to disconnect" laws, many people find themselves worried about work, checking in, and answering emails when they ought to be spending time with family, relaxing, and enjoying life. Many people wish they could give that all up, but they would still need to support themselves somehow, which makes a selfsufficient lifestyle very attractive.

## *Back to Nature*

As described above, people have lived on homesteads for thousands of years, since the advent of agriculture. Many people feel "wrong" living in the city, as if they're missing out on something. One major motivation for living on a homestead is getting back to nature and living a simple life deep in touch with the land. This kind of lifestyle can be rewarding and many people take a great sense of pride in being able to support themselves with the environment around them.

Furthermore, sustainability is a major concern for many homesteaders. Many people want to ensure that they are doing everything they can to prevent the climate crisis from deeply altering our world by switching to sustainable methods of energy and food production. When done correctly, the homesteading lifestyle can be very sustainable. For example, growing food on site cuts down on one's carbon footprint by eliminating the  gas needed to transport food to a grocery store from a large-scale farm.

# Self-Sufficient Living

Living off the grid can be a very enticing lifestyle for those seeking more freedom and independence. This means producing your own electrical power, collecting and pumping your own water, and growing your own food. It's not a very common lifestyle. However, many people these days prefer to live independently and to minimize their reliance on fossil fuels. While some people choose to go completely off the grid, others may prefer to go partially off the grid and still rely on the central systems for electricity, gas, or water. There are many advantages to living away from the city. However, not all countries allow this kind of lifestyle. So, here is a self-sufficient living guide to help you get started.

## What Is Self-Sufficient Living?

First, let's go over the definition of self-sufficiency and the main factors contributing to living off the grid. Self-sufficient living is the ability to become the producer and provider for your own daily needs. This includes building or creating your own shelter and getting your own food that may come from the land around you or animals you own. So, one of the main aspects of self-sufficiency is owning a land big enough to hold your home and animals. Another big part of the process is knowing how to maintain your off-grid system and support your home and family. This may also include reaching the required mental stability level that allows you to face large-scale challenges. Doing that will allow you to enjoy the life you have worked to build.

Finally, you need to know how to get yourself out of debt so that all your energy is dedicated to maintaining your off-grid lifestyle. Living out of the city does not require a lot of money, but you still need to save enough for emergencies and put all your money to good use instead of paying interest.

**Getting Rid of Debt**

The first steps you need to take to go off-grid begin when you're still living on-grid. The first thing you need to think of is money, and although you can go off-grid without saving, you first need to work on going debt-free. You also need to accumulate a little bit of cash in order to build a safety net for when you go off-grid. Start by calculating the amount of money you regularly spend every month, then gradually pay off any pending debts before making any preparations. There will always be creative ways by which you can cut expenses and save money. Aim to downsize your requirements and train yourself for living outside the city. Even if it's not to save up and pay off your debts, it's crucial to teach yourself how to live on minimal essentials before making a move.

That being said, let's get into what self-sufficiency is not.

Basically, self-sufficiency is not living as a consumer. You have to rely completely on yourself to provide for your own needs. It's not using dietary staples, animal food, land fertilizers, or any other resources that do not belong to you. Self-sufficiency is not about depending on the grid to let you accomplish your daily chores or tasks. It is also not about self-isolation and turning your back on the community that exists around you. It's more about providing for yourself and knowing that your needs and demands are still met even when community resources cease to exist.

Self-sufficient living does not include depending on purchased canned or dried food without the ability to refill them yourself. You need to understand that problems can be solved without the help of professionals. You need to get everything you might need without waiting for the sympathy of others. You are the one and only provider, and nothing can stop you from being selfsufficient.

So, in a nutshell, self-sufficiency is the physical and mental resilience to all needs. It's about changing your identity and going from a consumer to a producer. While it may be easy to explain in writing, it can be a lifelong journey to understand the concept.

## Off-Grid Living

Apart from the mental and physical aspects of living off the grid, this lifestyle allows you to become less reliant on some principal pillars in the conventional on-grid culture. Let's go over them one by one to find out how to substitute them and experience a true self-sufficient lifestyle.

## Electricity

The first and most prominent thing you have to give up when you live off the grid is electricity. You need to be completely independent of the main electric grid. This can be done through various methods. Some people live without electricity, some rely on one or more generators, while otherss choose to produce their own electricity by depending on alternative energy sources such as the sun or wind.

## Water

Giving up water means disconnecting from the water grid and finding an alternative source that would allow you to build your own water system. Many off-grid homes rely on lakes to provide them with drinking water.

## Natural Gas

This means giving up gas used to heat homes and run stoves.

## Sewer

The sewage system is the part most people forget about before switching to off-grid living. Instead of relying on the main sewer system, you will need to look for an alternative. This includes outhouses, field beds, septic tanks, and composting or propane toilets.

## Advantages of Self-Sufficient Living

### Increased Self-Dependence

One of the best benefits of living off-grid is achieving full self-reliance and learning how to handle yourself in case of societal collapse. You'll learn a great lesson on independence, and you'll be able to master the nature around you. When you live outside of society, you'll be forced to harvest your own food and fulfill your own energy needs, which will teach you to depend on yourself in every aspect.

## More Interaction with Nature

If you are ready with all the necessary all-season equipment and gear, it's guaranteed that you'll enjoy your time outside all year round. Living off-grid is all about spending more time outdoors and connecting more with nature. When you choose this kind of lifestyle, you'll understand how wilderness is the true giver of life. You'll eventually find yourself spending the majority of your time outside, either harvesting food, looking after your land, or simply just relaxing and enjoying the weather.

## Creating an Eco-Friendly Lifestyle

You can make a significant impact on the environment just by switching to an off-grid lifestyle. Think about all the electricity and fossil fuel power you'll be giving up on by disconnecting from the grid. When you switch to self-sufficient living and rely on renewable energy like solar power and wind power for your daily needs, you significantly reduce your carbon footprint and help develop a more sustainable society. You also learn to invest in the best durable gear that is more likely to last for years instead of contributing to the wasteful throwaway culture.

A More Affordable Lifestyle

While the initial costs of living off-grid can seem a little high, you'll be saving up thousands of dollars in the long run. The initial costs are usually the most expensive since you will need to build a home, set up an electrical system, and invest in durable gear and supplies. Regardless, you'll be saving up a lot of money that could have otherwise been spent on utilities, food, and superfluous expenses.

Now let's take a look at how you'll be able to save money on utilities.

- Solar Power

If you go with solar panels, you'll make a huge positive impact on the environment and save yourself a few thousand dollars every year. Solar power is very affordable now, and it helps homeowners save up a lot on electricity bills. You can even use solar panels to cover a small portion of your daily electrical needs while relying on generators for the rest of your power consumption.

- Battery Storage

Battery storage prices are currently coming down to a very affordable level for homeowners. There are many innovative products nowadays, such as the Tesla Powerwall, which is both durable and affordable.

- Electricity Prices

As the current electricity prices are increasing due to many factors such as new grid costs, network infrastructure costs, and the general increase of wholesale electricity prices, you'll be able to save a lot of money if you go off-grid.

## Disadvantages of Self-Sufficient Living

Anything you do will have its advantages and disadvantages. However, it's always best to stay prepared for any downfalls you may come across. Here are a few cons of self-sufficient living to keep in mind.

### Initial Costs

While living off the grid may be one of the cheapest lifestyles, it costs a lot to get started. You'll first encounter the costs of constructing your own home and whatever other utility-alternative systems you need. You'll need to afford your own land and set up a water system for drinking and washing. The gear you buy at the beginning of your switch will also cost you a lot, given that you'll need some long-lasting supplies to help you combat the outdoor environment. It will be quite an investment. Whether you choose a solar power system or any different method, the costs of power will also be quite high. Since cutting these costs won't really be helpful, it would be better to choose your initial investments wisely.

## Roof Space Limitations

Depending on the size of your house, your roof space may not be sufficient for the number of solar panels you need to power your home. In fact, the size of the roof you have over your head is one of the most important determining factors when it comes to meeting your home's electrical needs. If your roof is not large enough to fit the number of solar panels you need, consider opting for ground-mounted solar panels.

## Reduced Convenience

You'll have to make a few compromises when switching to off-grid living. Let's be honest, there will be no Uber Eats or a fast internet connection. You'll have to get used to the limited access to pharmacies, grocery stores, and even clothes and equipment suppliers. You'll also be disconnected from many professional services such as auto repairs, construction, land management, plumbing, and other common fundamentals.

## Unguaranteed Paybacks

Solar power systems may be affordable at the moment, with acceptable payback periods ranging from 3 to 5 years. However, battery systems are still not a good investment, and their payback periods have only recently been reduced to be shorter than their warranty periods.

## Backup Power Generation

When you go off-grid using solar power, you will need a system that can at least power your home or give you energy autonomy for 3 to 4 days. This means that you'll need a backup generator or battery storage system for emergency situations. Battery storage systems can require a lot of maintenance.

## Property Value

If you're changing to a self-sufficient lifestyle, you need to be prepared for a potential decrease in your property or house value. Some people may be looking forward to buying an off-grid house. However, many other people would look at this fact as a disadvantage rather than a quality. This is why you'll need to make some changes if you're planning to sell your house in the future.

## Loneliness

Most of the people you know probably live in a conventional society. While off-grid communal environments exist, you may not always be lucky to find one or live in one. This is why you need to be prepared to go weeks or even months without talking to anyone. You must be ready for some occasional loneliness if you're really considering self-sufficient living.

## Usage Spikes

You need to understand that even your regular solar power consumption can be exceeded any day throughout the year. If you have guests over at your house, you're more likely to consume more power than usual. This is why you need to plan your power usage and prepare for unexpected usage spikes.

## Self-Sufficient Living Tips

Now, the previous part may have all been about the difficulties of living off the grid, but apart from the advantages and disadvantages, some tried tips and pieces of advice may help make your life easier when switching to a selfsufficient lifestyle. Here are some of our best tips.

- Adapt to your new home and make your new environment work for you.

- Aim for frugality and living with the available resources or means you're given. You can't expect to switch to self-sufficiency while owing people money and refusing to pay your debts.

- Plan your food according to the season. You won't be lucky enough to rely on grocery stores, so you need to at least eat whatever is in season.

- Aim to create a homestead wherever your home is. This will help you grow your own food and raise the livestock you need to harvest food.

Location is Crucial

## Things to Consider

Sometimes, we don't realize how much of our lives are reliant on the grid. When becoming self-sufficient, a number of the things that we take for granted during city life are suddenly our responsibility. Below is a list of things to keep in mind when selecting a lot to build a homestead, or transitioning your current home to off-grid power sources. Ensuring your lot will be able to take care of each of your important needs in a practical manner is essential to establishing a sustainable, long-term homestead.

## Space

Homesteads vary in size, ranging from less than an acre to hundreds of acres. To ensure that your homestead can support you and your family, it needs to have enough room for your alternative energy methods, gardens, and animals. If you don't wish to become self-reliant in one or more of these aspects (for example, if you want to switch to off-grid power and water but are still okay with going to the grocery store for food), you can forgo some of this, but if you're becoming completely self-sufficient, you might need more property than you expect.

Some guides recommend at least 19,000 square feet per person when it comes to plotting out a garden for food. This translates to a little under two acres for a four-person household. This amount of space can be reduced by using vertical or hanging gardening techniques for vegetables. Animals also require their own space to be healthy and happy, which can increase the

space requirement to at least three acres. If you are using a
wood stove for heat, you want to ensure that your property has
enough wood. Thickly forested properties can sometimes have
enough wood on the ground that can keep your house warm
for some time without cutting anything down, but eventually
you'll have to harvest trees if this is your chosen heating
method. In general, ten acres of forested land is enough for you
to harvest wood for personal use indefinitely, without stripping
the property bare.

Isolation, Access and Communications

Living a solitary life in nature is the dream for many
homesteaders, but being isolated from society comes with a
tradeoff.

Consider the possibility of a medical emergency. Even if you're
young and healthy, accidental injuries and other unexpected
medical events can happen to anyone. Try and determine how
long it would take an ambulance to reach you in the event you
had to be rushed to the hospital. If you're uncomfortable with
the distance between your homestead and the nearest hospital,
choosing a property closer to emergency services can help you
to feel safer in your home. If you do choose a very isolated

property, knowing your coordinates, as well as how to direct emergency services to your homestead from the highway, could make the difference between life or death.

Getting *yourself* to your property is just as important. Many remote homesteads can only be accessed by a dirt road through a wilderness area. If this applies to your property, find out who owns the road and who's responsible for maintaining it. For example, knowing who will be responsible for clearing snow and filling potholes. In some cases, off grid properties are accessible by a road that cuts through the property of another person. In this case, you need to receive permission from the owner, or an easement from the courts, to be able to use it. An easement is a property interest that grants you to access another's property in a limited capacity, for one specific purpose. An easement would allow you to use a road to access your property if there was no other way to do so, but would not permit you to come and go from the neighboring property as you please.

Communicating with the outside world is also something to take into account. Consider whether or not you'll be able to have internet access at your homestead, as well as cell service or a landline. Being able to communicate with the outside world is a safety issue, as you need to be able to call for help in an emergency, but keeping in contact with family and friends is also important. Loneliness can have a negative impact on your mental and physical health, making it harder to stick to your lifestyle in the long term. You can also use the internet to find important information in a pinch, such as how to fix a broken piece of equipment, or how to find other homesteaders to socialize, barter, and share information with. Furthermore, having access to the internet may be a necessity if you choose to work from home to make money off the grid.

Finally, it is important to learn who owns the properties around yours and what they are used for. If the properties nearby are zoned industrial or up for development, you may want to look elsewhere. You don't want to build a homestead in a scenic forest, only to have it surrounded by industry or urban sprawl in a few years!

## Children and Homeschooling

Many people choose to homestead to make a better life for their children. They recall playing outside and getting muddy throughout their childhoods, and want the same kind of experiences for their children as they grow up. Today, in an age where most children grow up with a device in their hands, this kind of valuable free-range play can be hard to come by. However, homesteading with children presents a number of concerns that should be considered before you sign the deed on a property.

Children have a right to an education and making sure your kids get schooling is an important part of preparing them for adulthood. Obviously, commuting several hours to a school from an isolated homestead might not be feasible five days of the week. Homeschooling is a legitimate way to educate your children if you feel qualified to teach them, and can also allow you to teach your children in the way you feel is best for them. Homeschooling laws differ from state to state, so it's important to look these up before you design a curriculum and dive in. Some states provide a curriculum and may require you to maintain attendance records, or otherwise regulate the process.

Children love their friends and socializing with other children their age is vitally important for their development. If you have children, consider whether or not they will have access to peers outside of the family to play with on a regular basis. This is especially important if they are homeschooled. Enrolling your children in extracurricular activities such as sports or a church youth group can help them make friends outside of traditional public school. Finally, looking for homesteading groups in your area is another great way to find and connect with other like-minded families with kids! Areas with strong homesteading communities are more likely to have active groups, so keep this in mind when selecting your location.

Climate

Whether you choose to homestead in the USA or abroad, the climate of your region can make or break your experience. For example, while there is an active homesteading community in Alaska, the brutal winters of the region can come as a shock for newcomers who are unprepared. On the other hand, the extreme summer heat of many regions of the South, while normal for locals, can be difficult to cope with for people from out of state. It's recommended to try to visit a new state if its climate differs significantly from what you're used to before committing, preferably during different seasons of the year. If this is not feasible, an alternative could be to talk extensively with locals or people who've spent time in the state about the climate.

Along with regular weather patterns, natural disasters should also factor into your choice of location for your homestead. It's worth looking up what natural disasters your chosen area is prone to and whether you can sustain them at your homestead, or if you're better off looking elsewhere. Finally, it is crucial to consider whether the climate of your chosen region is suitable for growing crops. Depending on weather patterns, some states have longer or shorter growing seasons than others, and the temperature and moisture of the region can affect what crops grow best. It's important to do research on this before moving to a new state to homestead, or at least before planning out your garden.

Soil and Water

Closely related to the issue of climate is the quality of the soil and water on your homestead. This is more something to look into once you're considering a specific property rather than the state at large. The condition of the soil and water on your property determines if and how you'll be able to sustain yourself on the land, so this is the right time to be picky!

Companies exist that will collect soil and water from your property for testing, or send you appropriate tools and containers to collect it yourself. Soil and water can be contaminated by chemicals from nearby industry, or runoff from nearby farms. In order to determine if this is a risk, consider the properties around your homestead: who owns them, and what are they used for? Undeveloped land could be converted into large-scale farms, so knowing who is buying the surrounding property can protect you from investing your homestead in an undesirable area. If you're lucky, there will be a body of water on your property like a lake, river, or stream, though these can really increase the price of a piece of land. Be very cautious about relying entirely on a natural body of water for your water supply, as these can dry up unexpectedly and aren't always full throughout the entire year. Doing some research on the body of water in question and how it's affected by the seasons can ensure that you won't be left looking at a bare lake bed with no alternative. Learning about nearby properties is important in this case as well, as it can inform you if there is any history of pollution, such as dumping in a lake. Finally, most states allow you to collect water from natural sources on property you own, but some states have laws that restrict how much you can take, or what you can use it for. Be aware of your local regulations before starting to keep yourself out of legal trouble.

Surface water isn't always the best way to get water on your homestead. The vast majority of the Earth's freshwater is actually hidden in underground springs, and digging a well can help you access it. Ensure this water is tested for contaminants before using it, and always treat both surface and groundwater with a UV filter before drinking to guarantee it's potable.

If the soil and water on your homestead are unsuitable for growing crops, your property may still be suitable for homesteading. For example, some homesteaders choose to have a tank put in and filled with water from outside the property, though this can be inconvenient. Rainwater collection, while usually not reliable as a main source of water, can also be used to top up onsite water tanks. Raised beds and container gardens, which are filled with outside soil and compost, are ways to grow crops on a property where the soil is less than fertile.

## Food Supply

While this is closely related to the section above, how you're going to supply yourself with food is something to consider before you commit to purchasing a lot. Not only do different regions vary in climate, making certain types of crops more viable, but they also have different laws that could make it easier or harder to grow food on your property. For example, animal agriculture is often regulated by local zoning laws, which could prevent you from having chickens, pigs, or other livestock on property.

Depending on how remote your property is, you might be able to dip into the local grocery store for supplies regularly. But, if you're more remote, this becomes less convenient. These considerations are important to factor into your location selection. People who live on remote properties may also look to the land around them for the food it offers. Hunting, trapping, fishing, and foraging are all very ancient ways of getting food, but are subject to your local laws and regulations. For example, licenses for harvesting animals from the wild are required in all states and vary in how much they cost.

Butchering farmed or hunted animals is also a skill that requires practice to achieve, and if you choose to raise or hunt your own meat this is something you'll want to learn. Some homesteaders have successfully taught themselves these skills using online tutorials to butcher small animals like chickens and porcupines, but if you want to hunt or raise larger animals, you will need inperson guidance to learn how to do this properly and with minimal waste.

Power and Heat

To avoid getting sick, it's important that your living space on your homestead stays insulated from the elements. Furthermore, even though you're moving out of the city, you may not want to give up every modern convenience. Most homesteaders produce some form of electricity on their property, usually from a generator, solar panels, or windmills. Each of these power sources have their own pros and cons when it comes to sustainability, cost, and longterm maintenance. For example, wind turbines cost a lot to set up, so it's important to be aware of whether your property gets enough wind to make it worth it in the long term. It might also be difficult to get zoning approval for wind turbines if your property is located at the edge of an urban or suburban neighborhood. Solar panels are not quite as expensive and subject to fewer regulations, but also present a significant investment. Propane generators are surprisingly efficient and cheaper to get your hands on, but require you to continuously purchase propane over time.

There are pros and cons for heating choices as well; popular choices include: wood stoves, pellet stoves, propane heaters, and more. Wood stoves and pellet stoves are very simple, easy to maintain, and relatively cheap to operate, but have more of an environmental impact when compared to other methods.

**Checklist: Is this the right property for me?**

- I can afford to purchase this property, as well as pay the required property tax and building permit fees, if necessary.

- I have a clear way to access the property. If I have to pass through another property to reach it, I have permission or an easement that allows me to do so.

- Emergency services are able to find and respond to this property if necessary.

- The soil and water on this property have been tested and are free from contamination.

- This property can support my chosen method of food production. There is enough space to grow food not only for daily consumption, but to store for the winter.

- If I'm using wood for construction or fuel, there's enough available that I will not strip the property.

- There is no risk of chemical, pesticide, or contaminate runoff from neighboring properties.

- Neighboring properties are not zoned industrial, or up for development.

- There is a clear and reliable way to obtain water on this property, or enough space for water tanks.

- Zoning restrictions do not prevent me from building, using alternative sources of energy, raising animals, or any other activity I'm planning to do.

- This property has, or can get, cell phone service, a phone line, or internet access.

- My children, if not homeschooled, will be able to commute to school.

- The location of the property allows me to find other families with children the same age as mine.

## Best and Worst States for Homesteading

In this section, we'll be going over the best and worst locations in the United States for homesteading, based on four specific factors. If you don't see your state among the "best places" list, don't rule out homesteading there! While these are particularly great states for homesteading, there are many places where you can live happily off-grid all around the country. Using the above checklist, as well as the traits of a good state for homesteading we've included below, do some research and see if your state measures up!

Before we begin, it's important to understand the meanings of a couple of terms.

A *homestead exemption* is a law that protects you from having your land taken by creditors during a financial crisis, so long as it is your primary residence. Homestead exemptions can only apply to one property and provide protection from creditors for amounts ranging from $5,000 to potentially hundreds of thousands more.

*Zoning laws* restrict what you can build in sections of a state or municipality. For example, zoning laws would prevent you from building a family home in the middle of a commercial area. These laws can sometimes get in the way of raising animals or other activities typical of homesteaders.

The states included on this list have been selected based on four criteria:

1. Climate and soil: How suitable is this state for growing crops? Is there a high risk of natural disasters that could destroy your homestead?

2. Laws and regulations: Will zoning laws be a major obstacle to setting up your homestead? Do laws restrict how you can homeschool your children? How easy is it to sell your produce?

3. Cost of living: Does this state provide a homestead exemption, and if so, how much? How expensive is it to live in this state? Is there a free land program underway?

4. Community: Is there a strong homesteading community in this state? How many local resources are available to you?

# Best States for Homesteading

## Tennessee

Tennessee has always been a strong agricultural state, with the growing season spanning nine months out of the year in some counties. There's no shortage of water in the state, you can harvest from natural sources and collect rain water, or tap into one of the state's numerous underground aquifers. With over ten million acres in Tennessee dedicated to farming, you'll have no trouble finding fertile land on which to start your off-grid life.

While the average cost of buying an acre of agricultural land in Tennessee has risen to $3,998 in recent years, don't let this turn you off. With thousands of listings available around the state, you're sure to find something within your price range. Property taxes are a low 0.64%. Along with a generous homestead exemption, you might be able to get a financial grant from the government if you're a homesteader who's fallen on hard times. If you want to sell products from your homestead in Tennessee, you can reach out to local organizations for advice in getting your business off the ground. You will also have no trouble finding a homeschool group in your area. This security and support network makes Tennessee very attractive for homesteaders who are just starting out.

The law in Tennessee specifically allows you to homestead anywhere in the state except for urban areas. While the laws surrounding homeschooling are not as permissive as those in some other states, you have a number of options for educating your children, including online schools and church-run umbrella schools. If you prefer to teach your children yourself, you're required to show that you have education equivalent to a high school diploma, and submit records of attendance as well as standardized test scores.

*Idaho*

Idaho is home to tens of thousands of homesteads, and has a strong homesteading community presence both in person and online. Along with the fertile soil and green landscape, the laws in Idaho are perfectly suited to the independent homesteader.

The soil in Idaho is lauded for its fertility, and the moderate climate of the state is perfectly suited to growing crops. While winters are much more wet and humid in the northern part of the state in comparison to the eastern part, you can expect 18 inches of rainfall per year in most of the state, with some regions receiving much more. Between this and abundant lakes and rainwater, there is no shortage of water in Idaho.

Idaho's homestead exemption is one of the highest in the country, with 50% of the value of your home and up to $100,000 protected from creditors in the event of a financial emergency. This exemption does require you to file a Declaration of Homestead in order to qualify, so keep this in mind if you want to minimize your interaction with government entities. On the other hand, Idaho allows you to homeschool freely and develop your own curriculum.

The median cost of buying a home in Idaho in 2021 is higher than the national average, at $348,483, in comparison to $231,200 as of 2020. However, other aspects of cost of living are lower, including insurance and property taxes, meaning that moving to Idaho can still be worth the investment. The price of agricultural-zoned land is valued at $4070 an acre in 2019.

*West Virginia*

West Virginia is a beautiful state with a low cost of living and a strong farming community; in fact, most farms in West Virginia are family homesteads! The laws of the state heavily favor independent homesteads, and the low cost of living makes this south-east state a viable option for any frugal homesteader.

If you're homesteading in West Virginia, collecting rainwater is a very promising option for contributing to your water supply. This fertile state gets up to 44 inches of rain a year, and boasts high rainfall in the middle of the summer. Along with rainwater, there's no shortage of underground aquifers, which contributes heavily to the popularity of off-grid living in the state. The very permissive homesteading laws also allow you to collect water from lakes and rivers on your property.

Cost of living in West Virginia is up to 22% lower than the national average, making this among the cheapest states to live in. Property taxes rest at a very low 0.57%. The price of buying a lot, home, or homestead in West Virginia is much lower than in other states, sometimes less than half of the national average, and there is no shortage of options. A cursory review of websites where off-grid rural properties and homesteads are bought and sold reveals thousands of active listings. The homestead exemption, which can only be applied to one property, protects $20,000 of the value of your homestead.

Laws in West Virginia specifically protect homesteaders, allowing you to build freely on property you own without stressing about zoning. While you need to register for a business license to sell your crops at this state's many farmer's markets, the $30 fee will be waived. However, stricter laws surround homeschooling, requiring you to declare your intent to homeschool, submit a curriculum for review, as well as complete records of progress and attendance.

*Kentucky*

A full 50% of the land in Kentucky is classified as farmland, and the state is home to tens of thousands of farms, including a thriving community of homesteads and family farms. This state has a cost of living 16.4% lower than the national average, making it an attractive choice for the economical homesteader. Property tax rate is 0.87%, and the average price of an acre of agricultural land is $3920.

Winters in Kentucky are relatively cold and may dip below freezing. However, the overall climate of the state is mild and temperate, with plenty of rain at 45 inches a year on average. There are also many underwater aquifers and lakes that provide irrigation to the region's vast farms and pasturelands. Thanks to the warm and humid climate, the growing season in Kentucky is long, so you'll have plenty of time to garden and fill up your pantry before winter sets in.

Thanks to the agricultural industry in the state, you'll have no trouble purchasing livestock, or finding resources to help with setting up a garden. You can also sell most products from your homestead without a license. The 150 farmers markets scattered across Kentucky  make it easy to find a place to set up your stall.

While not as permissive as others on this list, laws in Kentucky aren't much of a barrier to setting up a homestead. While zoning limitations do not restrict where you can homestead in Kentucky, you will need a permit to build or modify the buildings on your property. Homeschooling laws are relatively relaxed, and you can homeschool freely as long as you maintain attendance and performance records, and ensure your children meet the state's graduation standards.

*Oklahoma*

Oklahoma is a warm south-central state boasting almost 80,000 farms. With the third lowest cost of living in the United States, and cropland going for a low $3160, Oklahoma deserves the consideration of any economical homesteader looking for a new home. As agriculture is the backbone of the state, as with those listed above, the laws and climate in Oklahoma are also suited to homesteaders who value their ability to support themselves and their families on their land.

Oklahoma has a property tax of 1% annually, but there are no taxes on purchasing land, reducing the strain of the initial cost. Homestead exemptions are available for $1,000 off the value of the property.

Furthermore, there are a number of farming organizations present in the state which are able to provide a beginner homesteader with advice and resources as they get their new life off the ground. Thanks to the popularity of homeschooling in the state, there are also plenty of groups that can help you ensure you meet the state's requirements. Homeschooled children in Oklahoma must be instructed at least 180 days a year from the ages of 5 to 18, and must receive an education on par with the state's curriculum.

While the climate in Oklahoma varies, the state is known for its fertile, welldrained soil that is suited to growing both summer and winter crops. Seventythree percent of the water in the state is groundwater, so digging a well is a prime option in Oklahoma. Some regions get up to 45 inches of rain a year, so rainwater harvesting isn't off the table in certain counties. There are plenty of livestock markets and farmers markets that make it easy to buy and sell.

## Worst States for Homesteading

### Florida

While the soil in Florida can be great for growing crops, and the state does have a booming agriculture industry, don't pack up for the Sunshine State just yet: there are a number of reasons that you may be better off going elsewhere if you want your homestead to be successful.

Land in Florida gets quite expensive at $7,190 for cropland and $5,360 for pastureland, as of 2019. You would also need to register your farm with a number of government entities, such as the Department of State, the Department of Revenue, the IRS, and potentially, the Department of Agriculture and Consumer Services. The Department of Citrus might also require registration if you grow certain fruit crops. Furthermore, you need to seek a number of permits from the Department of Environmental Protection. You'll have more freedom to live the way you want to by looking for a state with less bureaucracy and restrictions.

Another major factor in making Florida one of the least attractive states for homesteaders is that, with the rise of climate change, Florida has become a common place for hurricanes to make a landfall. The high winds and flooding associated with hurricanes can destroy a homestead very quickly, ruining the years of work and thousands of dollars you put into it. Extreme weather events will only get worse as climate change progresses, so a homesteader with an eye to the future is better off looking somewhere else.

*Hawaii*

The gorgeous island state of Hawaii is a prime tourist location, but the small amount of land available and the massively high cost of living make it nearly impossible to homestead there successfully.

As Hawaii is an archipelago, many goods need to be shipped there from the mainland, resulting in increased prices. The cost of living in Hawaii is 73.6% higher than the national average, and a single acre of land can easily go for $870,000 or more!

While you can technically lease farmland from Hawaii's Department of Agriculture at a rate of $200 an acre annually, this isn't a loophole that would allow you to homestead freely. Not only do you have to be a previous resident of Hawaii for three years or more, and have previous farming experience, you need to submit financial information to show that you are capable of running a for-profit farm. You're also not permitted to live on the property. Unless money is absolutely no object, and you're happy living offsite, you'll probably be crossing Hawaii off your list.

*Nevada*

Thanks to the dry, arid climate, farming in Nevada is usually more trouble than it's worth. With 3400 farms as of 2021, only 8.7% of land in Nevada is agricultural. You'll have a lot of trouble finding high-quality land for farming if you choose to homestead in this state. Water is in relatively short supply, and the lack of a strong homesteading community makes it harder to find support and resources.

Nevada is relatively expensive to live in, but many people raise an eyebrow at the low price of land. With acres going for as low as $1,050 in some counties, frugal homesteaders might be tempted to give this state a look. However, you get what you pay for; much of the land for sale in Nevada is unsuitable for farming or raising crops. If you're looking to sustain yourself off your land, you're better off looking elsewhere.

*California*

As California produces much of the nation's produce, some would be tempted to think that setting up a homestead there would be easy. However, this West Coast state presents a lot of obstacles to potential homesteaders.

The main issue with attempting to homestead in California is the climate. California is prone to droughts and these will only get worse with climate change. You don't want to find yourself wondering how to distribute limited supplies of water among the crops, animals, and people on your homestead. Furthermore, the chronic droughts in California bring something even more dangerous with them: wildfires, which can very easily destroy a homestead you've worked hard to build and maintain.

The price of land in California can get outrageously high, at over $12,000 for a piece of pasture land. The law also requires you to apply for a license to run a working farm, which means disclosing a vast amount of personal information and documents. You will also have to obtain a license to sell crops at a farmer's market, and what you can sell is limited. Overall, while it's not impossible to do successfully, homesteading in California is expensive, potentially dangerous, and bogged down by laws and bureaucracy.




## Options for Your Off-Grid Living Space

Traditional Houses: From Dry Cabins to Modern Models

When most people think of a homestead, they picture the homesteaders living in a simple log cabin or small cottage most of the time. While this isn't the reality for many homesteaders, these types of simple dwellings are still popular among many, but can come with drawbacks.

A "dry cabin" is a simple structure not fitted with any kind of running water or plumbing. While dry cabins can sometimes be wired to municipal or offgrid electricity sources, the term is mostly used for cabins without modern amenities. These homesteaders make do with pit latrines and simple wells or natural water sources for these needs. People who live in dry cabins usually cook over an open fire or wood stove. This is the most difficult kind of homesteading, as your need for firewood and water don't go away when you're tired or it's cold outside. Before committing to this kind of lifestyle, you need to be sure that you'll be able to keep up with the demands. People who choose dry cabins are usually experienced homesteaders or outdoorspeople who really crave a challenge. Dry cabins are also used in Alaska and other regions where extreme cold temperatures make indoor plumbing a challenge to maintain.

When living in a dry cabin, you'll have to retrieve water manually from your natural source, well, pump, water tank or storage shed, and carry it into the house for use throughout the day. One way to do this is to place a five- or ten-gallon jug with a spigot in the kitchen and fill it up at the beginning of the day. If you want hot water, you'll generally have to heat it up on the stove and then pour it into whichever appliance you're using. Having electricity opens up your options for water heating, but without plumbing you're still limited.


Log cabins are one of the most common types of dry cabins. If you have a knack for carpentry, you can purchase a "log cabin kit" which you can assemble yourself. These come with all the materials needed with detailed instructions, and go for $18,000 to $40,000, or more. Some companies have an additional charge to ship the wood, fasteners and other materials to your properties, so check the fine print to see if this applies to you.

If dry cabins don't appeal to you, building a house or cabin that provides more modern comforts, like a connection to off-grid sources of electricity and water. This is one of the most popular routes that homesteaders go, as it allows them to plan their home according to the conditions on their lot and what needs are important to them.

DIY-ing your modern living space is an option if you have the skills and knowledge needed to do so safely, otherwise it's highly recommended to seek help from a professional! This is doubly important when it comes to wiring lights and electrical outlets; doing this wrong can be very dangerous. If you don't have the necessary skills to build a house on your own, you will likely have to hire someone else to do it, incurring an additional cost.

A ranch style home is a one-story house with an open floor plan, usually on the smaller side, that is very popular among homesteaders. According to the building site Fixr.com, the price for building a ranch style home is usually at a minimum of

$104,000 for a simple one-bedroom, including labor. If you're able to build your home yourself, you can get the price significantly lower. The price for building a small two-story home, by contrast, ranges from $93,000 to $175, 000.

Tiny Houses

Tiny houses pack the comforts of a traditional home into as small of a space as possible. Like traditional houses and cabins, they can be very simple or fully equipped with modern amenities. The main advantage of a tiny house is that you don't need a huge property to set one up. They range from less than 150 square feet to the maximum of 800 square feet. Tiny houses are often fabricated off-site and fitted with wheels to be transported to you, before being placed on a regular foundation or staying on a movable trailer. If you have a small property, living in a tiny house can save you a lot of space for gardening, solar panels, or anything else you have planned. You could also potentially set up more than one on your property if you wanted to create a multi-building layout.

Since their power requirements are smaller than most regular houses, tiny houses are also well-suited to alternative forms of energy such as solar. Many DIY solar panel kits are suitable to power a tiny house, and can be set up on the roof or on the ground nearby.

However, the cons of tiny houses are also directly related to their small size. If you're using solar power or another form of alternative energy, you'll have to find a place in the tiny house to keep the battery consistently above freezing temperatures to protect it from damage. With limited space, this can be a challenge.

Furthermore, most people who live in tiny houses spend most of their days outside and this can get uncomfortable if you live in a colder region. While tiny houses are suitable for homesteads where 1-2 people live, larger groups and families will find the lack of space harder to manage. Even loving families need personal space and alone time!

Tiny houses range from approximately $30,000 to $60,000 to build, making them one of the most cost-effective options for your homestead's living space. However, if you're building your home yourself, using recycled materials, and forgoing add-ons, you can get the bottom line down much lower. A significant portion of the price of building a tiny house goes to insulation, which can add up even for the smallest homes. Don't even think about skipping this investment; insulation will prevent you from spending a fortune on heating and cooling your home later on!

The cost for affixing solar panels to the roof of a tiny house is about $3,500. Similarly, to log cabins, you can buy a tiny house kit that comes with instructions to help you to do it yourself. These can range from less than $4,000 to $50,000, or even more in the case of a very high-end home. Either way, you'll save on labor costs by using a kit.

Prefabricated Homes

Prefabricated—or prefab—homes are getting more popular among modern homesteaders, and it's easy to see why. These homes are designed and built off-property and then transported to your homestead to set up. While there are different types of prefab homes, two of the most common are *manufactured homes*, which are fully or mostly assembled on a trailer and then moved to your property, and *modular homes*, which are built in sections off-property, then assembled with a crane on site. The majority of the benefits of prefab homes come from their convenience.

Higher-end prefab homes either include sustainable utilities such as solar panels or modern compost toilets, or have the option to add them in. A cursory look over the websites of successful prefab home retailers show that they can also help with things like well and septic hookup. Therefore, buying a pre-equipped prefab home can save you time and money, depending on the model you go with, and allow you to have the modern amenities you value. It removes any questions from setting up regulated or skilled amenities like power, water, and sanitation by bringing in professionals with skills and experience.

However, there are downsides to prefab homes. The first is the cost. Prefab homes can get quite expensive, especially if you're purchasing customizations or add-ons like high tech composting toilets. On the other hand, there are prefab homes that cost much less than a traditional home. Don't forget, you may have to pay for the home to be transported to your property, though some companies waive this fee. As you're purchasing your whole home as one product, you also have fewer options for the layout than if you designed it yourself. Most prefab retailers have a range of models available for purchase and may accept customizations for an additional charge.

The ZeroHouse, one of the most high-tech modular houses in the market, costs $350,000. On the other hand, modular homes can go for as low as $50,000 or less, but at this range your options are very limited, only covering home delivery and materials and not add-ons like septic tank setup. Prices at the lower end of the range also don't cover labor.

Manufactured homes are cheaper in most cases, with small, simple models ranging from $48,300 up to $109 300 (TheBalance, 2021). Manufactured and mobile home loans are available to help you finance your purchase, and it's worth shopping around to different lenders to see what types of loans are available.

Mobile Homes and RVs

Recreational vehicles and mobile homes combine a lot of the pros and cons of the previous types of dwellings. While these homes can be cost-effective and have the added benefit of mobility, their small size can be a limiting factor.

Mobile homes and manufactured homes are often conflated, and while they are similar, there are key differences. Mobile homes are dwellings built in a factory setting before 1976. While people are still buying and selling these dwellings, remember that they were built before many of the modern safety and quality standards we're used to today were in place. Due to the outdatedness of mobile homes in comparison to modern manufactured homes, you might feel more secure buying a more recent model. It can be very difficult to get a loan on these homes because of this liability. Furthermore, mobile homes are stereotypically flimsy, and many of them are still on wheels. Mobile homes were meant to remain mobile and potentially be moved to different rental sites over the course of years, while manufactured homes are intended to be moved once and are often placed on a foundation. If you see a mobile home for sale and are considering moving it to your property, have it inspected before purchase (this is required by law in some states). An inspection can alert you to any unseen flaws or safety issues with the dwelling.

On the other hand, more and more homeowners are setting up RVs— recreational vehicles—as their off-grid dwellings. RVs are large trailers usually fitted with a sleeping area, a kitchenette, a bathroom, and a sitting area. While intended for use in travel for recreational purposes, these lowcost vehicles can be renovated to become your permanent house. If you're buying brand new, a medium-sized RV starts around $10,000. Secondhand is considerably less. Modifications can add some additional cost, but if you're getting creative with your DIY skills and recycled or found materials, you can turn an RV into a comfortable home for relatively cheap. People who have retrofitted RVs into comfortable homes spend between $500-3,000 on renovations in most cases. Changes made to RVs can be as simple as painting and replacing furniture, or get as extensive as remodeling the entire interior and adding additional appliances.

Alternative Housing: Container Homes and More
Homesteaders are very creative. In recent years, we're seeing more and more alternative housing options turn up throughout the internet, and some are ingenious. Usually, these plans involve creating a home out of something intended for another purpose, like a shipping container. Using innovative plans can save a lot on the cost of materials and labor.

When creating an alternative living space using these materials, it's important to remember that you become responsible for ensuring that your home has everything it needs, since it won't come with anything in place! On the other hand, if you're a crafty person, you can really use this opportunity to create a custom living space that is truly your own. We'll use shipping container homes here as an example, but people have also successfully converted prefab outbuildings and grain silos into off-grid homes.

Shipping containers are relatively cheap, going for as little as $1,000, but you don't want to buy at the lower end of the price range: these shipping containers may be decades old, rusty or damaged, or too small. Remember, the container will be a lot less spacious when everything's inside. A highcube shipping container in good condition is the best for turning into a home, as the extra foot of headspace makes it easier to add insulation and flooring. You can make a bigger home by buying several shipping containers and putting them together. A used high-cube, 40-foot shipping container goes for approximately $2,950, while a new one costs about $5,800. Not bad in comparison to the other prices listed above, but remember that modifications need to be made.

Once the shipping container is on your property, it needs inside modifications before it's fit to live in. The floor of the original container is often treated with chemical pesticides and needs to be replaced with cement, wood, or other flooring that suits your preference. Furthermore, insulation needs to be added to ensure you don't bake in the summer and freeze in the winter. Expanded foam insulation is one of the best options for shipping container homes. The insulation is manufactured off-site, shipped to your site, and then installed by professionals or by yourself using stud attachments or glue. An added benefit of expanded foam insulation is that you can get corrugated varieties intended to match the shape of shipping container walls. The average cost of expanded foam insulation is $1.73-$3.67 per square foot.

## Budgeting for Your Homestead

So how much does it cost to go off the grid? As you've seen, land and dwellings vary wildly depending on your region, the additional costs of setting up the power source, food supply, water supply, and more can really build up. While we're unable to give you a solid number due to the differences between the states, some estimations are included here. The following section should be used as a guide to determine how much it'll cost to build a homestead in your specific circumstances.

Homesteading is a great investment when done right. The more self-sufficient you become, the less you'll have to spend monthly, but there is a significant entry cost. Furthermore, you'll also need to budget for unexpected situations, such as a failed harvest.

However, homesteading is most feasible for people who are in a good financial situation. If you don't have money to invest in setting up your homestead, you have a much higher chance of failure as time goes on. It's strongly recommended to be completely debt-free and have good credit when you start your homestead. Some tips for saving additional money would be to cancel any subscriptions you don't need, avoid eating out, and purchase reusable products whenever possible.

Overall, the entry cost of homesteading, when it comes to acquiring land, a livable home, garden, animals, water, power, and sanitation infrastructure, is much higher than you might expect. $50,000 to $150,000 covers a dwelling in most cases, including labor, materials, and equipment. While you can technically homestead on just a couple acres of farmland, recall that enough quality land with access to water and fertile soil can get quite expensive. Some homesteaders pay $25,000 to $100,000 or more for an appropriate lot, though paying close attention to listings can help you luck out on something much lower. On top of this, you'll have to budget for additional equipment and materials for later projects, such as your garden and livestock and outbuildings.

While many aspects of this list can be financed in order to relieve the immediate financial burden, it's worth calculating the total costs to determine whether you'll be able to comfortably afford the transition.

## Checklist: Costs of Off-Grid Living

- Land: $25,000-150,000+

- Dwelling: $50,000-150,000

- Small shed: $600

- Garden set up: $500-2,500

- Livestock: $100-$5,000 for the animals

  - Chicken coop and run: $100- 1,000

  - Barn or shelter: $25-65 per square foot

  - Barbed wire fencing: $1-6 per foot

- Energy:

  - Solar panels: $1,000-30,000

  - Wind turbine: $41,500-124,500

  - Batteries: $200-300

  - Back-up system for batteries: $7,000

  - Propane generator: $500-11,000

  - Propane (per year): up to $18,000

- Water and Wells

  - Geotechnical survey to locate groundwater: $1,000-5,000

  - Dug well: $1,000 or less

- o Drilled well: $15-100 a foot, average cost of $5,500

  - o Pump and plumbing: $2,000

  - o 1000-gallon cistern: $500-1,000

  - o 55-gallon food grade drum, secondhand: $100

- Sanitation:

  - o Pit latrine construction: $100-1,500

  - o Modern compost toilet: approximately $1,500

  - o Septic tank setup: $1500-5,000

  - o Septic tank pumping and cleaning: $300-600

- Expected expenses: $1,000/month for additional supplies and repairs

## What Might Your Homesteading Lifestyle Look Like?

Example 1: High-Tech Homesteading

Jeff and Maria Fernandez are a married couple in their late thirties, with three children: Jim, 11; Anna, 7; and Blake, 4. When they started a family, they knew they didn't want their children to be raised by a computer tablet, but to grow up experiencing nature and the outdoors. They also desired to get back to nature together, spending more time as a family instead of commuting to and from work.

The Fernandez family live on a five-acre homestead 15 minutes outside of a small town. Both Jeff and Maria work from home to provide an income. Jeff is a freelance computer programmer, while Maria is a part-time online tutor, who also homeschools their children. In order to accommodate their work schedule and the children's schooling, they needed reliable power to their homestead to support their internet connection. Therefore, they set up a row of solar panels to provide power to the house and draw water from a drilled well that provides running water to the house.

Since they invested in modern water and power, the family's main chores surround their animals and garden. As they maintain a container garden, watering and weeding is required every day to keep their plants healthy and happy. During harvest season, much of the day is taken up by picking vegetables and fruits from the garden and preserving them by water bath canning and pressure canning. The family also feeds their free-range chickens twice a day, collects eggs, and occasionally butchers a chicken for meat. Thanks to their active participation in their local homesteading group, they're able to trade produce grown on site for meat from other homesteaders. The family enjoys foraging together in their free time.

Example 2- Keeping It Simple


Blake and Anna Murphy are a married couple who moved to a 12-acre forested lot in order to escape from the hustle and bustle of city life. As their region gets very cold, they chose not to invest in indoor plumbing for fear of pipes freezing and breaking in the winter. The Murphys live in a small dry cabin, where they use a propane generator to provide power to a few lights and appliances, including a chest freezer. They also use a propane stove for cooking. Most of the heat in their homestead comes from a wood stove, and they use a simple pit latrine for sanitation.

As there is no running water inside the house, the first task of each day is to ensure the 10-gallon jug of water in the kitchen is full by retrieving water manually from their well. While the Murphys maintain a large wood stockpile, harvesting wood from the forest on their property is a task they perform twice a month, as they can't afford to fall behind.

Anna and Blake have planted a number of crops on their property in raised beds. The growing season for warmer-weather crops such as tomatoes and peppers are short, so they grow more cold-weather crops like radishes, onions, potatoes, broccoli, and cauliflower. The couple use a fermenting crock and a water-bath canner to help them preserve their harvest. The Murphys derive most of their income from a mix of sources. Anna is a freelance writer, while Blake teaches classes on hunting through a local homesteading organization. They also allow people to camp on their property for a fee, allowing them to bring in some additional passive income. Blake hunts during the open season. A single large game kill can put plenty of meat in their chest freezer. The couple preserve their game meat by smoking or dehydrating it into jerky, and trade some with other homesteaders for honey, fruit, or other crops they don't produce themselves.

From the above two examples, you can see that the daily activities of homesteaders vary widely depending on which modern amenities they've chosen to invest in.

In a survival situation, the next most important thing after water and shelter is food. You can only survive for so long without food. If you are looking to live off-grid indefinitely, you will need some way of generating your own food. As we have seen in many scenarios, such as earthquakes, tornadoes, and even the recent pandemic, the food supply is severely impacted when global and local transport routes are blocked. If you are in a survival situation, going to the local grocery store may notan option, and even if it is, it won't be a long-term solution.

## How to Grow Your Own Food

The first option you have to create a long-term food supply for yourself and your family is to grow your own fruits and vegetables. There are so many different kinds of things you could grow that you could live nearly entirely off of. You could manage a piece of farmland just for farming, or you could expand your operations and even start making an income from it. In fact, even if you are growing on a small piece of land, the yield is often so large that people have to give some of the produce to other people, or it will spoil. For instance, if you grow lettuce, you will usually get a lot of it, even from just a small gardening patch in the backyard. As this kind of vegetable doesn't have a long shelf life, nor are there good ways to preserve it, you can easily sell it or share it with friends and family. Also, if you consider doing your own farming, you can use organic processes, which will yield better quality fruits and vegetables that can also be sold for a higher price. Let's look at some of the basic things you need to know about growing your own food.

Soil

Good soil is like a storehouse for all the things plants need to grow. It contains nutrients, air, water, and organic matter, and it also serves as a comfortable foundation for the plant to develop roots that support growth aboveground. Depending on where you are and your local conditions, your garden soil might be ready to use right away. However, you might need to do extensive repair work to get the soil in good condition, or you might have to add in completely new soil to get the space to a condition where you can grow things.

To rely on this long-term, you want to make sure that the soil is in top condition. Otherwise, you might not be able to get any benefit out of it after the first harvest. Good quality soil that has been properly maintained can provide you with an endless supply of food and is the basis of good farming.

Before you start planting or looking for the kinds of plants you can grow, it will be helpful to get a better understanding of the soil you have. Different areas have different kinds of soils, which will impact the kinds of fruits and vegetables you can grow and how well they will grow. If you don't have the right soil, you should invest in getting enough soil dumped.

In some regions, you might have very wet and oily soil because the surface has a lot of clay in it, while in other areas, you might have rocky soil with very little fine grain material in it. Some areas also have extremely fine soil that clumps up and forms a hard solid surface when dry. Ideally, you want a soil that easily crumbles, is dark, can hold a lot of moisture, doesn't have rocks, and won't harden into a solid surface.

## Basics of Soil Fertilization

Starting farming can be very difficult if you don't know the quality of the soil you are working with. There are a number of easily available testing kits that you can buy from gardening stores or farm supply stores, and you can check the quality of the soil yourself. If you are looking for a more in-depth solution, have a larger area to work with, or have the right soil but just need to know what it lacks, you can hire a professional geophysicist to test your soil and give you a report. The most important things you need to know about the soil you are working with include the pH level and the amount of magnesium, phosphorus, calcium, nitrogen, and potassium. These are the primary sources of nutrients that plants need the most to grow properly. There are a number of other secondary nutrients that plants also need, but this is not going to be too much of a concern if you are frequently adding organic matter and other energy sources to the soil. The most important thing you need to know is how alkaline or acidic the soil is or the pH level. Ideally, you want it to be between 6.5 and 6.8 on the pH scale. Anything below 6 (acidic) or anything above 7 (alkaline) is going to be too harsh for plants. Regardless of the nutrients in the soil, being too acidic or too alkaline makes it very difficult for the plant to draw them from the ground.

Once you have the right kind of soil, the next step is to improve its quality to maximize output. This involves giving the soil the things it is inherently lacking and providing it with the nutrients that are not readily available in the natural environment.

The first thing you need to manage in your soil is the amount of oxygen it has. Just like humans, plants need oxygen to survive, and more importantly, it is the nitrogen in the air that plants need to grow. Also, having enough oxygen in the soil will help other small organisms flourish, which plays a pivotal role in the life of plants. This is why you need soil with the right consistency to hold the right amount of air. If you have a very oily and claylike soil, the particles are too small, and when they clump together, they eliminate air. Sandy soil is the other extreme, as particles are too big, there is too much air, and plants cannot develop strong roots, and organic matter decomposes so fast that they don't have the time to consume it.

Adding compost helps maintain a good amount of air in the soil, and this is why you shouldn't step in it or use heavy equipment, both of which can compress the soil and squeeze the air out of it.

Next, you want the soil to have about 25% water. Getting the right amount of water is just as important as having the right kind of soil. If the soil is very dense, it will cause the water to pool around your plant, which will cause them to rot. If you just planted seeds, too much water will drown them, and they will never germinate. On the other hand, very porous soil will let too much water through too fast, leading to the plants not getting sufficient water to thrive. Again, adding some kind of compost will help in this regard and make it easier to manage the amount of water in the soil.

There are some kinds of pests such as caterpillars that are going to be bad for your crops. They eat leaves, fruit, and even roots. On the other hand, some other organisms will be beneficial and essential to maintaining a healthy ecosystem. Things like earthworms, nematodes, fungi, and bacteria are some of the few organisms that will help your plants grow. For example, earthworms help move the soil around, promoting oxygen flow and even helps release standing water.

When it comes to providing your crops with additional sources of energy, minerals, and vitamins to assist in growth, you have the option to either use completely natural products or naturally occurring materials. Considering that you will be using these crops in a survival situation, you might not have access to manufactured crop supplements such as packaged manure and other manufactured ingredients for too long. It's great to have some of these items stocked, as this will help you get the crops going initially, but in the long run, you will probably need to rely on natural sources.

There are many things that you can use to help your crops grow better, and you can use all kinds of things to create your own organic matter. You do have the option of purchasing store-bought organic matter, but there is only so much that you can store before you run out or it goes bad. One great trick you can use to get off to a solid start is to mix the organic matter with the soil when you are initially laying it down. This drastically improves the nutritional value of the soil, and you have a stronger base that will last you much longer in the years to come. Natural compost and organic matter help your soil retain more water and absorb nutrients. Also, things like compost are a great source of energy for smaller microorganisms, which helps drive the ecosystem.

An easy way to create your own organic matter is simply to pile on brown and green layers. Brown layers include straw, cardboard, and dried leaves, and green layers include waste food, livestock manure, and green grass. All you need to do is make sure it is moist and to keep rotating it often to help break it down faster and more evenly.

You can also use a combination of organic or artificial mulch to assist your crops. Organic mulch includes shredded bark, sawdust, hay, grass clippings, and other kinds of natural waste material. Layering mulch over the crop field helps reduce evaporation and protects your crop field in extreme weather conditions. It can also significantly reduce the growth of weeds and limit the number of infestation of undesirable pests. As this organic mulch slowly breaks down, it provides the ground underneath with all kinds of nutrients and minerals and also helps retain water better.

Inorganic mulch will include small pebbles, gravel, landscape fabric, or even plastic sheets. Artificial mulches provide some protective benefits of regular mulch, but they don't provide any additional nutrients. More importantly, these kinds of mulches do not need to be replaced every year, and you can use a sheet of plastic for several years. However, these are great if you are looking to improve the quality of the soil.

Further, there is the option to use fertilizer to assist in the growth process of your crops. This will include everything from dry or liquid fertilizers to natural or artificial fertilizers. Generally speaking, natural fertilizers will be slower to release their nutrients, but act for a much longer period, whereas artificial fertilizers will be fast to act but only for a short period. Also, natural fertilizers will not have any side effects, whereas, with artificial ones, you always risk the possibility of killing off the microorganisms that help your crops grow.

## Storing Seeds

For some plants, it will be really easy to store the seeds and use them in the future. You need to save the seeds from the fruit or the vegetable and store them properly. It can be a little harder for other plants that have a male and female plant and require cross-pollination to germinate. In the case of crosspollinating plants, it will be easier to have store-bought packs of seeds as these are already prepped, and you can plant them right away.

The wind helps to cross-pollinate some plants, and bees and other similar insects also help with pollination. For things like corn, it can get a little tricky to ensure that your crops aren't cross-pollinating. While this won't affect your current crop, the seeds you use from a cross-pollinated crop will not be very good in terms of quality. They will still yield fruit, but it just won't be as good as a pure seed.

Crops such as tomatoes, beans, peas, and peppers are self-pollinating plants. All you need to do is dry out the seeds and store them in an air-tight container, or you can store them in a paper envelope with a small sachet of silica gel to ensure that they don't develop any moisture and go bad. If you don't have silica gel, you can also use powdered milk to act as a desiccant. Simply take a tablespoon or two of milk powder and place it in a cheesecloth or a tissue and tie it up and place it into the container or food-grade plastic bag and it will draw out any moisture. If you are using milk powder, make sure you replace this every six months, or it can start to go bad as well. Also, make sure you label each bag and write down the date of packaging. Ideally, even though they can last several years with proper storage, you should use your seeds within a year. The only drawback is that the longer you store the seeds, the lower the germination rate becomes.

Irrigation

When it comes to formal farming and commercial irrigation systems for large crops, there are many solutions that can be used, from highly sophisticated drip irrigation systems to common and easy-to-build canal irrigation solutions. The problem is that these solutions rely on a good supply of water, and they also require some mechanical and technical expertise to use and maintain. For instance, if you installed a drip irrigation solution for your farm and sprung a leak or broke a drip nozzle, it's not going to be very easy to repair. Therefore, for survival farming, your irrigation solutions will be dictated by the kind of water supply you have and the terrain you are planting in.

To make your farming a bit more manageable, it will really help to have a level field to plant your crops. At the very least, you want some flat areas, and if you can't plant all your crops in one area, you can spread them out and have small patches in different areas.

In this scenario, it will become possible to create a canal irrigation system where you carve out a canal that flows through the major portions of your land. When you flood that with water, you can use a bucket to move the water around the different areas of the plantation. Also, if there is a stream nearby, you can create a channel from the mainstream and divert that towards the main canal on your field, and this will give you a constant supply of water. You can build a small dam on the main channel, which will help you regulate the amount of water the plants receive.

The other solution is to build a watershed. You can dig out an area in the land where you can collect rainwater or store water from a nearby source and use it to water your plants. Also, keep in mind that different kinds of crops have different water requirements. If you are planting regular garden vegetables, you might do just fine with regular rain, but you will need proper irrigation for more demanding crops such as corn and wheat.

**Perishables vs. Non-Perishables**

When planting your crops, you want to consider how well the fruits or vegetables will last in your environment. Things such as tomatoes, lettuce, and apples don't have a very long shelf life, especially in a hot climate. More importantly, you want to grow the food you can use right away, such as fresh vegetables, and some things that you can easily store and use when supplies are thin. For instance, things such as wheat, beans, lentils, barley, and corn, can be easily stored without a lot of processing, and they remain usable for quite a long time. These non-perishable items can be a bit more demanding to grow, but they are well worth the effort during winter when nothing else can grow in an open environment.

## Food Storage

This leads us to the bigger problem of general food storage. Other than the things you grow, you will also have fresh meat that you hunt, and you might also have other products such as fresh milk. When it comes to storing food, there are a few different options you can go for.

## Cellar

Cellars, also known as root cellars, are a fantastic solution if food storage and food preservation are a part of your plan. While these are mostly known for storing wine, the low temperatures and consistent moisture levels are ideal for storing a whole lot of other things as well. Cellars will be a little difficult to build, but if you can, you can store vegetables, fruits, and meats for much longer than you would be able to on the surface. Also, if you are going to be using pickling or drying techniques, the final product from these processes will also age much better in a cellar.

## Salting

Salting is probably the oldest method for preserving food. This is because salt naturally dries food as it helps extract moisture and kills many microbes that cause food to rot. However, you must understand how to salt your food because too much salt can be dangerous. Also, you need to know how to use salted food. It isn't as simple as easy as washing off the salt and eating the meat or vegetables.

## Drying

If you enjoy beef jerky or dehydrated mangoes, then drying food is going to work well for you. The great thing about drying food is that not only does the food last much longer, but it also intensifies a lot during the drying process. When you use dried food, such as dried tomatoes, you only need to use a little bit to get a good amount of flavor. This is another method that works great for meat, vegetables, and even fruit.

## Pickles

Pickling your food is also a good way to preserve it, but it does take a bit more work and requires some additional ingredients that you might not always have. For instance, if you are looking to pickle your food in oil or vinegar, you will need quite a lot if you plan to store a decent amount of food that can support two or three people for several months. Also, this might not be the best option if you need to store meat or foods that can be consumed as a full meal.

## Jams

Jams are very popular today not just because of their flavor but also because it's a preserved food that can survive for long periods. The problem with jams, just like pickles, is that their flavor intensifies a lot over time, and it is a very cumbersome process. For example, if you are planning on making strawberry jam, you will need large amounts of sugar, and you won't be able to use it as the main source of food. You will most likely need to have bread or rice or something else to accompany it.

One of the best things you can do for yourself and the people staying with you is to raise livestock. Whether that is chickens, goats, or cows, having live animals is an invaluable resource. These animals will provide you with everything from food to clothing to protection and even transport. Again, it does depend on where you are and what the environment is like, but typically, animals such as horses, chickens, and lambs are extremely resilient animals that can withstand tough conditions. If you are in an area where you have access to more animals specific to that region, definitely go for indigenous breeds. These indigenous breeds will have adapted to the local environment, and their chance of survival will be much higher than any other animal. More importantly, animals meant specifically for farms, such as cows that have been modified to produce as much milk as possible, are very difficult to manage. They have very specific dietary requirements, are very sensitive to their surroundings, andare completely helpless if they don't have humans caring for them.

Also, you don't need to have a lot of animals to start with. You can easily start with just a few chickens and a couple of cows or a couple of horses, and they will breed and grow over time. Animals such as chickens and goats breed very quickly, and they multiply in numbers every season. The larger the animal is, the slower its reproductive cycle is, but they offer unique benefits. Horses are a fantastic animal to have as they can help you move items, plow, and water the land.

Dogs are also a good animal to have in a survival situation. They can help you hunt and protect your territory. When hunting wild boar, deer, or even birds, dogs are very useful to have around.

Other than dogs, you don't have to worry too much about feeding your livestock. If you have enough vegetation around, your animals can graze on their own. Once you show them a good source of water, they can take care of their food and water needs. Of course, providing them with water and food will help them develop, but even on their own, they will manage just fine. Dogs will need food, but they can easily survive on kitchen scraps.

The three main things you will get from livestock are eggs, milk, and meat. Once you have enough animals, you can use some for your own consumption, which will be very important, especially in the tougher parts of the year.

If you are considering getting livestock, it is a good idea to get relatively older animals. Raising small animals, especially animals such as chicks or baby horses, can be a lot of work. It requires some special tools and materials that will not be easily available in a survival situation. Older animals are usually ready to reproduce and you don't have to wait for them to reach maturity. This means you can start developing your flock as soon as you get them. It might take them a few weeks to adjust to the environment, but sooner or later, your animals will start to multiply.

If livestock seems like something you would be interested in, you must develop a shelter for them. This could be a large barn that all the animals share, or it could be separate housing for animals to live in. However, if you want them to multiply, you will need to give them proper housing to lay their eggs or give birth and keep their young ones protected in the initial few weeks.

## Water

Collecting from Natural Sources

Why dig a well when you could draw water from a river that rolls right through your property? While collecting water from a natural source seems like the easiest solution to securing your water supply, in reality, it's not that simple. Many homesteaders do rely on a natural source for water, but there are a number of things to consider first to make sure it's safe and practical to do so.

Health and safety experts, such as the Wyoming Health Department, strongly recommend having surface water sources tested for contamination at least twice a year, and again any time you notice a change in taste, smell, or appearance. Water testing is usually conducted by a private company that will send you a pre-approved sterile bottle with a stabilizing agent included. You'll collect the sample on your own, following their instructions, and return it to the company for testing.

If there is no evidence of contamination, you still need to make sure that your water is potable before drinking it. Surface water is home to a wide variety of wildlife, as well as plant life and bacteria. A coarse filter is used to remove sediments from surface water, as seen in common gravity filters. You should also treat the water with UV light to kill off any bacteria or mold. Furthermore, this is another situation where checking your local laws for deciding on a water source is important. While most states allow you to collect water from a lake or river on your property for personal use, others restrict this if the water is going to be used for agriculture.

Wells

In the distant past, people noticed that when they dug into the ground at certain places, the bottom of the hole would be filled with water. The deeper they dug, the more water would fill the hole, allowing them to continue drawing water for months, years, or even indefinitely. Therefore, the concept of a well was born, and people have been drawing water from underground sources ever since.

There are a couple of terms you need to understand before we get into our discussion of wells, both of which are defined briefly here.

An *aquifer* is a reserve of freshwater that exists beneath the earth's surface. The vast majority of freshwater in the earth exists underground, and much of it is found in these. Think of aquifers not as caverns in the ground filled with water, but water-saturated regions in the soil and porous rock. The goal of digging a well is to penetrate an aquifer in order to pump or draw the water out.

The *water table* is the place where, when you're digging, you start to hit earth that is saturated with water. The water table is the surface of the region where enough water exists in the ground to easily pool at the bottom of a well. If you continue digging past the water table, you'll find that the space between the soil and inside porous rocks is completely filled with water.

The great thing about wells is that with groundwater, you'll be getting much cleaner water than surface sources can usually provide. The purity of groundwater is the reason people have been successfully using it for thousands of years. However, it's important to make sure you don't *introduce* contamination to your well water by letting water run into the well from the surface. Ensure that your well is securely covered when not in use, and that in the event of heavy rains flooding won't spill into the well. Build your well at least 30 yards, preferably more, away from your sanitation infrastructure as well as any lakes or rivers. Even with these precautions, filtering and treating your well water is strongly recommended.

A geotechnical survey can be used to determine where on your property the groundwater is located. These usually cost between $1,000 and $5,000.

## Dug Wells

When you think of a stereotypical well, you're probably thinking of a dug well. These are the type of wells that people have received water from for thousands of years and are still in use in many regions throughout the world today. However, there are numerous downsides to using a dug well that might make them more trouble than they're worth.

Typically, a dug well is simply a deep hole in the ground, dug by hand or with a small amount of machinery. A wall is put around the opening of the well with a roof or cover on top to stop debris and people or animals from falling in. With most dug wells, water is drawn by hand, usually using a pulley system to make the process of lowering and lifting a bucket easier.

Using a bucket whenever you need water is a lot of work especially when it's cold, wet, or stormy. Having water stored on property can negate this to a certain extent, but you'll still be drawing water by hand on the regular. Consider the climate of your region while deciding if this is the well you want to make.

The biggest concern with dug wells, aside from the manual labor involved, is that they could potentially dry up with time, as they rely on a single, shallow aquifer. You may need to re-dig a dug well over the course of the years, depending on how deep and reliable it is.

Despite the low cost of dug wells, it's recommended to have a drilled well with a pump on most homesteads, as this can save your property in the case of a fire. Because of the regular manual labor involved, most homesteaders choose not to rely on a dug well for their main water needs.

## Drilled Wells

As one of the most popular water options for homesteads, drilled wells are more reliable than dug wells because drying up is hardly a concern. These wells can extend hundreds of feet underground and draw water from a number of aquifers, instead of one close to the surface. Drilled wells also include a pumping system to get your water up to the surface; therefore, you'll also be doing much less physical labor than with a drilled well. Jet pumps can be used for wells of depth below 150 feet.

If you need more force, a submersible pump can be used to lift water up to 400 feet. A pump can be used to pump the water into a pressure tank through a supply line. This works much the same way that running water does on the grid, except you won't be paying the city every month for water!

The cost of drilled wells range from a few thousand dollars to tens of thousands, depending on a couple of factors. The cost of a drilled well depends on the depth, and is usually between $15-100 dollars a foot. Remember, if your homestead is situated on a hill, you'll have to drill through it to get to the groundwater, which can sharply increase the price. The average price to drill a well is $5,500, and can get as high as $50,000 in unusual cases. It may cost up to $2,000 or more for the pump and the plumbing required to supply your homestead with running water. A water cistern big enough for most homesteads' purposes can go for between $500 and $1,000.

In certain cases, you can get around the cost of a pump by looking into an *artesian* well. These wells function much the same way as other drilled wells, except that the water is brought to the surface by natural water pressure formed by groundwater entering the well. Whether an artesian well is feasible for you depends on the groundwater on your property, and a land survey can inform you as to whether this is an option.

*Driven Wells*

Driven wells combine some of the pros and cons of both the drilled and dug well. They are possible to DIY with the right materials or hire professionals. Driven wells are usually not much deeper than dug wells and lack some of the reliability of drilled wells in that they do not penetrate multiple aquifers. However, the convenience of a driven well can make up for the drawbacks.

Driven wells are made of a sharp "drive point" attached to a perforated tube, called a well screen, which is driven into the ground with a large mallet or machinery. Piping is attached to the well screen to bring the water up to the surface by use of a pump. This is a very simple explanation of the concepts behind driven wells, but more detailed instructions on how to build them can be found for free online.

One potential problem with driving a driven well yourself is that you can hit a rock during the driving process. You'll know if this happens when the pipe stops moving when you hit it. Don't keep hammering to try and force it, as this could ruin the drive point and well screen. Unfortunately, hitting a rock means you'll have to pull the tube out and try again somewhere else.

Driven wells typically extend 30-50 feet into the ground, and parts are available online to purchase. You can obtain the drive point, well screen, couplings, and pipes required to build a driven well for less than $1,000 in some cases, but keep in mind this doesn't include labor, the pump, and any machinery that might be used in the process. While driven wells are appropriate for having a convenient source of water on your property, for purposes such as irrigating crops or watering animals, they won't provide as much water as a drilled well. For fire safety, it's strongly recommended to have a drilled well with a pump on your property.

Many homesteaders take advantage of the rain to supplement their water supply, but if you're looking to do this properly, certain safety precautions should be in place to avoid getting sick.

Rainfall is measured in vertical inches, therefore, the more surface area you use to collect rain, the bigger your harvest will be. Simply placing buckets out in the rain will have very disappointing results. Looking around your homestead, you might notice that the roof of your house and barn has plenty of unused surface area. Gutters are placed along the edge of the roof to direct water as it rolls off and a storage container under the gutter spouts collects it. However, this method only works for a smooth roof, like a steel roof; regular shingles result in debris such as leaves, dirt, and bird droppings in the water tank, allowing bacteria to proliferate wildly. While this is a problem with steel roofs as well, they can be more easily hosed down between rainfalls. You can also fit a filter to the end of your gutter (don't forget to clean or replace this regularly!) and/or a first-flush diverter, which will divert the first portion of rainwater away from your tank or barrels. This allows the rain to give your roof a rinse, and leads to less dirt ending up in your water.

The price of a large water tank for storage runs between $500-1,000, and of course, the water falling out of the sky is free. First flush diverters can be purchased on Amazon for $76.65, while gutter filters are sold in packs of four for $16.65.

Remember that just like surface water, you'll need to filter and treat your rainwater to ensure it is potable. Many people choose to use rainwater for non-drinking purposes.

It is not recommended to collect rain as your main water source, as rain is not always reliable. Remember that weather patterns are getting more uncertain as climate change progresses! As we saw above, contamination is also a higher risk than with other methods. However, collecting rain can be a great way to get some extra water to irrigate your crops, and thus can be a valuable sidekick to your main water collection method.

While it's generally legal to collect rain for your own personal usage, some regions restrict this. Look into your local laws before getting started to avoid getting hit with a fine.

If all else fails, some homesteaders buy water and bring it to their property to be stored in large tanks, which may be located underground, in a shed, or even affixed to the roof of the house. This method does not require the homesteader to have a viable source of water on the property, vastly opening up their options for potential lots. However, there's a tradeoff in that driving or towing a large water tank off property and bringing it back regularly can be a major hassle. Furthermore, disaster preparedness is a concern for many homesteaders, and this method could become impossible in the case that something happens to the water grid. These large water storage drums or tanks can also be used to collect rainwater, so some homesteaders combine these two methods to reduce how often they need to fill their tank.

Finally, some homesteaders take a combined approach where they stay on municipal water while producing their own power and/or food. This isn't possible in the most remote properties, but can be an option if your homestead is located on the edge of a suburb, or is otherwise close enough to a town. Another reason to do this would be to plan to take one aspect of your life off the grid at a time, staying on municipal water until you've secured your power generation method off the ground, for example.

**Storing Water Safely**

It is always recommended to have water stored in the case of an emergency, be it a natural disaster or simply a problem with the water supply. The Center for Disease Control and Prevention recommends storing at least one gallon of water per person per day for at least two weeks. Remember that you'll also need to store water for your garden and animals!

Water in regular plastic jugs doesn't last forever because plastic breaks down and picks up bacteria over time. To store water safely, it's recommended to use a dedicated water storage drum that is specifically designed to keep your water safe over long periods of time. The price of a 1,000-gallon storage drum for water ranges from $500-1,000.

You can also use a secondhand food-storage drum for water storage if you want to cut down on costs and don't need a full 1,000 gallons. These come in a variety of sizes, though the most common is 55-gallon. Be absolutely certain when you select a storage drum that it is food grade—not industrial grade—as you want to be sure it was not used for storing harmful chemicals that could leave contaminating traces. Also, don't use a food storage drum if it was used for juice or dairy products, as these could also leave trace amounts to become a breeding ground for dangerous bacteria. A 55-gallon secondhand food storage drum sells for approximately $100.

Store your water in a cool place away from your sanitation infrastructure, as well as propane storage, or other potentially harmful substances. A basement, cellar or dedicated storage shed can all be viable options for storing water. A small prefab storage shed costs approximately $600.

**Checklist: What Are My Daily Water Needs?**

This checklist is a handy guide for determining the daily water requirements of a basic homestead. Remember that water requirements increase in hot weather and that your personal need may vary depending on what amenities your homestead includes!

- People (per each family member):
    - Drinking and cooking: 4 gallons/day
    - Shower: up to 20 gallons/day

- o   Flushing toilet: 4-8 gallons/day

  - o   Dishes: 8 gallons/day

  - o   Laundry: 20-30 gallons/load, depending on your method

- **Animals:**

  - o   Chickens: 3 gallons/day for flock of 25

  - o   Goats: 3 gallons/day each

  - o   Dairy cows (lactating): 35 gallons/day each

  - o   Beef cows: 4-20 gallons/day each, depending on weight

  - o   Pigs: 8-20 gallons/day each, depending on weight

- **Gardens:**

  - o   70 gallons/day per 1,000 square feet

## Power and Electricity

One of the biggest decisions you'll make when it comes to your homestead is how you'll be generating power. While some homesteaders choose to go without power, or with very limited power, most of us still want some of the comforts of modern life. The main three options for power on a remote homestead are solar power, wind power, and propane generators.

Solar Power

Solar power is one of the most popular methods, and it's not hard to see why. Solar panels do have an initial cost that can look steep to some, but over time, they pay for themselves.

Solar panels for homes are made of photovoltaic (PV) cells, which are made of semiconducting material encased in protective glass. PV cells are connected together in panels, which are mounted to face the sun (the angle of the solar panels depends on your region and altitude). A tracking system to tilt the panels over the course of the day to soak up the most possible sunlight is a part of many solar panel setups. PV panels convert sunlight to directcurrent energy and that energy needs to be inverted to alternating-current energy, which can then be wired into your home appliances, outlets, and the system's battery. This is done by an additional module called an inverter.

Solar panels are appropriate for homes that get plenty of sunlight each day.

As many of the states most suited to homesteading are located in the warm Southern USA, you can really get the most out of your money with this method. Solar panels come with ratings that show you how much power they provide under "standard" conditions, which refers to a clear day with plenty of sun, but in actuality you'll be getting less power than that as conditions will not always be perfect. Different regions of the USA have a number rating between 2.2 and 6.8 that can be multiplied with the solar panel rating to estimate how much energy that power would produce a day. Maps are included on the websites of most solar panel manufacturers. If a solar panel is rated 100W and you live in a region rated 3.5, that panel would produce 350W a day. An average solar panel system for a family home produces 8-10 kW a day.

How many solar panels you need depends on your energy consumption, as well as how much sunlight your region gets. Approximately 25-30 panels would be required to power the average home in America. It costs about $1,000 to have a single solar panel professionally set up, and approximately $30,000 to set up enough to power the average American home. Alternatively, DIY solar panel kits are available that can cut down on pricing by excluding the cost of labor. Solaris, a company that sells solar panels that can be set up by the homeowner, states that their average system (a tiered 8 kilowatt rooftop system) costs $11,059.98. While both of these options aren't cheap, as of 2021, US law provides a tax credit of 26% of the cost of the system for solar system owners as an incentive to encourage people to adopt solar energy. Therefore, your average professional and DIY solar setups would in effect cost between $8,184 and $22,200.

Batteries are used to power your home when the sun isn't out. They are charged by the solar power system during periods of sunlight. New batteries cost $200-300, and you'll also need a back-up system to accompany them, about $7,000. Batteries wear out as time goes on, so expect to replace them every few years depending on your power usage.

Wind Power

Wind power is appropriate for fewer properties than solar power is because it requires sufficient space and climate conditions to work. They can get more expensive than a solar power system as well. Despite the high costs, many homesteaders find their wind turbines are worth the investment.

Setting up a wind turbine is an option in areas that get regular wind speed of 12 mph or more. You also need enough space around the wind turbine to ensure that it gets the full strength of the wind: the blades should be approximately 30 feet above nearby trees and buildings, and at least 492 feet away from large obstacles. Furthermore, wind turbines can get very loud, and you want yours to be placed at a minimum of 328 yards away from your home. For this reason, wind turbines aren't suitable for smaller properties. But if you live in a windy region—and you own a large property—a wind turbine can be a viable option.

Wind turbines come in a variety of sizes, and a 5 kW to 15 kW turbine is appropriate for most homes. Wind power costs much more than the average solar panel system, between $41,500 and $124,500 for the entire setup, including the turbines and battery, delivery and labor. Like a solar panel, you'll need to connect your wind turbine to a battery to fall back on when the wind isn't blowing. Other wind turbines are linked to the grid when there isn't enough wind, but this option is less popular among homesteaders for obvious reasons!

One credit to wind turbines is their durability; a well-maintained system can last 20 years or more. A potential downside not related to the cost is that wind turbines are restricted by zoning laws in some states, especially if they can be seen from a public roadway. Do some research to see if this applies to you!

## Propane Generators

If sustainability is one of your main concerns, don't shy away from propane! Even though it is a byproduct of petroleum refining, propane is an efficient source of fuel, producing a lot of power per gallon, making it cheaper than a gasoline generator in most cases. Propane also burns relatively cleanly, with a long shelf life, making it much safer to have around than a gas generator.

In order to fully power your home with a propane generator, you'll need one that produces enough energy to match your daily needs. While generators are cheap to acquire compared to solar and wind power, there is a regular cost of purchasing fuel. A 13 kWh whole-home generator costs about $3.90 to $4.60 per hour to run. If you run your whole-home propane generator for 12 hours a day, 365 days a year, this adds up to a very pricy $17,082 in energy costs a year. For this reason, many homesteaders lean more towards solar or wind power, which have a large initial investment but pay for themselves over time, or use a combined approach.

Some homesteaders choose to use alternative methods such as candles and wood stoves for heat and light, and only use a smaller propane generator to run a limited number of appliances and to charge devices. It's also popular to have a generator as a backup source of power in case of a problem with the solar or wind system, or to power a few select devices. Along with 13 kW models, propane generators come in a range of power levels, including, but not limited to, 3.5 kW, 6 kW, and 12 kW models. Setting up a whole-house generator costs $6,000-11,000, including about $3,000 to purchase the generator. It costs $500-4,000 to obtain a small portable generator that you can manually turn on in an emergency. You can also get appliances that are powered by propane, allowing you to operate them separately from your electricity. Propane stoves, for example, are extremely common appliances on modern homesteads. A propane stove costs between $30 for a small oneburner camp stove to over $300 for a more sophisticated model.

A large propane generator is powered by fuel stored in a secure tank, which is usually installed underground. Companies that deliver and install propane generators also install these tanks, and you can set up recurring propane deliveries with them to keep your generator running. The cost of a 500-gallon propane storage tank (purchase, delivery, and installation) runs between $700-$5,000.

Safety note: Running a propane generator or stove inside will fill the space with carbon monoxide gas, which is odorless, colorless, and *deadly*. Never run your generator within 20 feet of the dwelling. If you use propane appliances, a carbon monoxide detector inside the house is a must.

## Sanitation

Surviving in an off-grid setup is not the easiest thing, especially if you don't know much about maintaining proper sanitation in your environment. Sanitation can be the difference between surviving and dying in extreme selfsufficient living emergencies. When you're living on your own, you will be subjected to all kinds of challenges. Some of them will be easy to prepare for, while others will be unexpected until you encounter them. Your personal hygiene and that of the environment around you can be a serious matter of health. You can easily fall at risk of contracting serious illnesses when you're not aware of the overall cleanliness of your place.

Now, whether you're prepping for surviving in an off-grid environment or already living a self-sufficient lifestyle, this guide will help you maintain good health by using the best hygiene and sanitation practices.

## Stock on the Right Supplies

Good planning is very important for preppers and off-the-grid homesteaders. To really plan and prepare for disaster, you have to make sure hygiene is on your list. This means that you need to stock up on the required supplies before living outside of the city and giving up on pharmaceutical supplies and grocery store items. Start by making a list of everything you need for basic hygiene and go shopping. Make sure you cover everything from house cleaning supplies to shampoos and other personal hygiene items. However, you'll need to decide between necessary items and luxury items. Living offgrid is all about saving money and spending the most minimal budget every month, so be careful not to overspend.

Your list may include things like hand sanitizers, shampoos, tampons, deodorants, soap, wet wipes, and all the other items you can't sacrifice or live without. Remember that you may have a limited storage space depending on the size of your off-grid house, so make sure you only include the items that are 100% necessary for good health and good hygiene. The goal is to increase protection, not to stock up on lavish products. This may mean giving up your hair conditioner or your expensive deodorant spray. Some people may even use soaps that double as shampoos. It's all about finding the balance between emergency preparation and saving money for a challenging, less convenient lifestyle. However, make sure you don't skip essential items such as first aid supplies and hand sanitizers.

## Find Clean Water

Having a clean supply of water is not just important for good hygiene. It's also one of the most important aspects of living off-grid. You will need to make sure you have more than one source of clean water before making or finalizing your plans to go off-grid. The part you need to start with is how you're going to store water for immediate use in case of a crisis. This can be achieved by either stocking up on clean water bottles or using your bathtub to store clean water.

In most cases, a water well will be the best option. So, before moving or considering self-sufficient living, aim to find a location where you can easily dig a well. It will be ideal to use well water for personal use. However, having a clean water stream nearby is also a good idea since it can be a great backup. Just don't rely on it. Having a well next to your home is always safer. It may also be smart to keep a few rain barrels filled with clean water for emergencies. The more water you have, the better. On the other hand, if you don't have enough water for cleaning, your health and hygiene will suffer.

Bathroom Preparation

Using the bathroom while living off the grid can be dangerous if you don't have your own septic system or working plumbing. This is because your or your family's waste needs to be properly dumped for sanitary reasons. However, no need to worry. If you're not lucky enough to have working plumbing, you can use a few other options.

One of the most sanitary options is digging a pit toilet behind your house. If this sounds like a solution you would opt for, make sure you have plenty of sawdust on hand so that you can use it to cover up the feces after you're done. Lime is another fantastic option to keep the pit clean and sanitary. Make sure you sprinkle some lime every time you use the pit. Some people may have toilets within their off-grid homes that don't have running water. If you're one of these people, you can use the toilet as long as you have enough water in your supply to flush down the waste every time you use it.

Another factor to consider is how you're going to use toilet paper. You can always stock up on toilet paper rolls. However, you'll eventually run out of them, so it's important to find an alternative. For most people, any type of paper can do the job. You can also use leaves, but make sure to stay away from poison ivy. It is also that you and everyone that lives with you wash your hands. Even if you don't have running water, opt for alcohol-based hand sanitizers or sanitary wipes to keep your hands clean.

## Personal Cleanliness

Personal hygiene is always possible as long as you have enough water. Of course, using the stored water to clean yourself is never as easy or as comfortable as hopping in the shower, but it's doable. It will be ideal if you have a river or a pond near your house so that you can take your baths there, but remember to use biodegradable soaps to avoid adding any unnecessary chemicals to the natural water. If you don't have a clean water source next to your house, you can always use camp showers to stay clean and maintain your hygiene.

Solar showers are a good idea. Simply fill the tank with clean water, hang it on a stable tree branch, and leave it to warm up. You can then simply open the nozzle to enjoy a warm outdoor shower. Despite that, the real issue is cleaning your dishes and making sure you get rid of all germs and bacteria. This is when an electric dishwasher is really handy in the city, as these devices really help sanitize eating utensils, and we take them for granted. However, when you're living off-grid, it will be necessary to heat the water you use for cleaning the dishes. Make sure you use enough soap and that you gently rinse the dishes in a light bleach solution. This step is particularly important for sanitizing eating utensils, especially if you live with a larger group of people.

## Other Areas of Sanitation and Personal Hygiene

Aside from clean water, bathroom supplies, and personal hygiene, there are many other areas to consider when taking care of your off-grid sanitation. For example, don't forget about the freshness and whiteness of your teeth. There will be no dental care when you're living outside of the city, which is why you need to stay ahead of any dental problems by flossing and brushing your teeth every day. Running out of toothpaste is no excuse for letting your dental health go downhill. You can always find alternatives. Living in the wilderness teaches you to be creative. Salt and baking soda are ideal for scrubbing and rinsing your teeth afterward. They will help whiten your teeth and keep them clean. People even used to chew sticks in the past, and surprisingly, it worked. It is also wise to find something fragrant enough to freshen the smell of your breath and clean out little bits of food when you chew it.

When it comes to menstrual cycles, you will need to stock on sanitary napkins or tampons to survive in an off-grid environment. They won't last forever, but they will support you until you can find a suitable reusable rubber cup for long-term use. These cups work perfectly for capturing blood, and they last for years. Make sure you wash your menstrual cup thoroughly after each use. Aim to store it in a concealed, dry container in order to keep it sanitized and clean. Wet wipes, both regular and antibacterial, are very important when prepping for a disaster. They are helpful when it comes to practical hygiene, so, if possible, have separate storage space for wet wipes. You need to have enough for face washing, hand washing, disinfecting, and between-showers refreshers. When you have the right items and supplies, you manage to maintain your health and stay clean even in the midst of disasters.

Washing Your Hands, the Right Way

Keeping your hands clean is crucial. A few important steps need to be followed when you're cleaning your hands to prevent potential illness.

- Get your hands wet using either clean running water or stored water.

- Cover your hands with soap or gently rub a bar of soap and massage your hands together, covering all parts. You should scrub your hands for at least 20 seconds before wetting them again or getting rid of the soap. Make sure you get the back of your hands, your wrists, under your fingernails, and between your fingers.

- The next step is rinsing your hands and thoroughly getting rid of all the soap.

- If you're using running water, use your elbow to turn it off.

Finally, you should dry your hands and make sure you don't touch anything unsanitary.

Taking a Shower

Many people may struggle to shower or clean without running water. However, there are always alternatives. There are many ways you can bathe or take a shower without access to running water. We mentioned a few techniques above, but what if you don't own a solar shower? What if your house is not near a pond or river?

Well, you can still give yourself a sponge bath using nothing but clean water and baking soda.

For this method, you'll need a large bucket filled with warm water and simply add about 3 tablespoons of baking soda to neutralize the odors of your body. Cover your hair with some baking soda water, scrub it gently, and then cover it with a wet towel. You'll need to refill the bucket for the next step, this time adding slightly less baking soda. Then, use a sponge to soak up some water and scrub your body with the mixture, making sure you cover all parts. You can use some soap for hairy areas to make sure you avoid odors.

Finally, rinse your hair using another bucket of clean water while scrubbing it with your hands to get all the baking soda out. Use a third bucket of clean water to rinse your body and remove any excess baking soda.

Baths are a great idea if you have enough water in your supply to fill up a bathtub, and of course, if you even have a bathtub. If you have both, fill up your bathtub with clean water and soap, then take your time scrubbing your body with a bath sponge to get rid of all the dirt. When you get out of the tub, make sure you rinse your body to wash off any dirty water.

Oral Hygiene and Health

These are all the tips you need to save water while brushing your teeth or using any other different method. This is also for people wondering how they can brush their teeth or use toothpaste without running water. Here's how it's done.

The most important part of brushing your teeth without running water is using a reusable cup. Some people even do it to conserve water and maintain non-renewable resources. Using a cup filled with clean water will help you rinse your mouth and get rid of the toothpaste. You just need to use all the water in the cup without wasting any. You'll also need a sink with working plumbing, a bowl to spit the water out, or any place where you can comfortably rinse out your mouth.

Make sure you use a clean and sanitized toothbrush and wash it after every use. Don't use your hands instead of a cup as this will waste a lot of your water supply. You should also remember to floss regularly. Just because you live outside of society doesn't mean you can let your dental health decline.

Feminine Hygiene Products in an Off-Grid Environment
For feminine products and menstruation, all you need is a reusable menstrual cup and clean water. Douching and feminine products, especially scented ones, are not really good for your health. You're only supposed to clean these areas with water and use tampons or menstrual cups to handle blood flow. Make sure you have a warm bucket of clean water during your menstruation days so that you're prepared. You can use wet wipes on the areas around your thighs, but all you need is clean water when it comes to the private areas.

Living off the grid means you're going to spend more time outdoors than indoors. This also means you'll be subjected to more open wounds and injuries. Unfortunately, medical assistance may not be available if you're living outside of the city. You must learn how to clean your wounds and sanitize them before they catch any bacteria. This is when sanitation can be the difference between surviving and dying.

For starters, you always need clean water to clean any open wounds. If you're outside and have no access to a water supply, some of your drinking water will do the job. You can also look for a river or any natural water source around to clean your wound and wash off any blood. The next step is sterilizing your wound, so you'll need a sterilizer or any other solution. If you don't have any sterilizer on hand, urine should do. You can also use surgical powder, but be careful not to apply any baby powder to your wounds.

Keep your wound covered after cleaning it, and make sure it's not exposed to any external elements. Any contact with dust or insects can cause infections, so use a piece of cloth to cover it until you can get home or have access to first aid supplies. If your wound is large and needs immediate covering, you can use plantain leaves as bandages as these leaves contain anti-bacterial and anti-inflammatory properties.

Taking Care of Babies When Living Off-Grid

Babies require a significant amount of attention under all circumstances. It's not very different in the wilderness. If you have a baby, you'll need to keep them clean at all times to prevent infections. In fact, babies should be given even more care and attention when you live off-grid. This means that you should change and clean their diapers more regularly. This includes times when they only pee. Your baby will be more prone to infections and bacteria when you live in a natural environment, as they will be more exposed to germs, dust, and unsanitary things. This is why you always need to have wet wipes on hand to prepare for unexpected emergencies. Make sure you find a clean area to change your baby's diapers. If you're outside, lay down a clean cloth to protect your baby from dirty surfaces.

## Getting Rid of Garbage

The final step is knowing how to dispose of your garbage or trash. You will need to start by sorting your garbage into four main groups: Biodegradable waste, metals and plastics, paper products, and sanitary items such as feminine hygiene products and diapers. Biodegradable waste, for example, can be composted by stocking it in a pile and dumped anywhere near your house, preferably in your backyard, if you want to use the waste for gardening purposes. Plastic items and metals require that you bury them somewhere away from your house, while paper products can be burned or recycled depending on your needs. Metals and plastics can also be recycled if you're crafty enough. Just make sure you cut back on your plastic use to protect the environment. Finally, you should dispose of any liquid waste by draining your garbage containers to avoid rotting, infections, and foul smells.

Sanitation is one of the most important aspects of self-sufficient living, as it helps you protect your health and avoid serious illness. To survive, you need to learn how to keep your environment clean and look after the hygiene of everyone living with you. Make sure you use the previous tips without overspending and wasting your budget.

# Conclusion

This book envisions a future where most of the world is thrown into complete chaos and disorder. This might seem like an extreme way of living for some people, but we can assure you that it is not. We hope that we have sparked your interest and shown you why prepping makes sense to some people who want to be safe and ready for whatever life throws at them.

The world we live in today is unpredictable and dangerous. We never know when something could happen that would make it impossible for us to leave our homes or find any of the things we need every day like food, clean water, medicine, etc. But with this guide, you'll have all the information necessary to keep yourself safe during an emergency. Prepping is a smart move. It's not just about preparing for the worst, it's about being prepared to survive and thrive in any situation you find yourself in. This book will teach you how to be self-sufficient and live off of your own resources even if society as we know it collapses around us. You don't have to be a prepper or survivalist to benefit from this book. Whether you want to learn more about prepping or simply prepare yourself for everyday emergencies, this guide has something for everyone.

www.ingramcontent.com/pod-product-compliance
Lightning Source LLC
LaVergne TN
LVHW050649200726
843506LV00010B/1433